Acknowledgement of Land & of the Traditional Owners of this Land

I would like to acknowledge the Gadigal people of the Eora Nation, upon whose stolen land I stand on today.
I recognise that this land was never terra nullius — the land belonging to these peoples was never ceded, given up, bought or sold.
I would like to pay my respects to Aboriginal Elders past, present and emerging, and I extend this acknowledgement to all Aboriginal and Torres Strait Islander people.

"The Don"
Is there anybody in there?

Comfortably Numb

"Hello? (Hello? Hello? Hello?)
Is there anybody in there?
Just nod if you can hear me
Is there anyone home?
Come on now
I hear you're feeling down
Well I can ease your pain
Get you on your feet again
Relax
I'll need some information first
Just the basic facts
Can you show me where it hurts?

There is no pain you are receding
A distant ship smoke on the horizon
You are only coming through in waves
Your lips move but I can't hear what you're saying
When I was a child I had a fever
My hands felt just like two balloons
Now I've got that feeling once again
I can't explain you would not understand
This is not how I am
I have become comfortably numb.
I have become comfortably numb.

Okay (okay, okay, okay)
Just a little pinprick
There'll be no more, ah
But you may feel a little sick
Can you stand up?
I do believe it's working, good
That'll keep you going through the show
Come on it's time to go.

There is no pain you are receding
A distant ship, smoke on the horizon
You are only coming through in waves
Your lips move but I can't hear what you're saying
When I was a child
I caught a fleeting glimpse
Out of the corner of my eye
I turned to look but it was gone
I cannot put my finger on it now
The child is grown
The dream is gone
I have become comfortably numb."

-"Comfortably Numb"
Songwriters: David Jon Gilmour/Roger Waters
Performed by: Pink Floyd

CONTENTS

1: Everything is Legal
(Tutto è Legale)
2: My Grandfather, Vito Martone
(Mio Nonno, Vito Martone)
3: Major Incident Unit
(Unità per gli Incidenti Gravi)
4: Mobius
(Möbius)
5: Lurking in the Shadows
(In Agguato nell'Ombra)
6: The Hermit
(L'eremita)
7: I Fought the System
(Ho Combattuto il Sistema)
8: Flatulate
(Flatulenza)
9: Do NOT Throw Food Away!
(NON Buttare via il Cibo!)
10: Live on the Edge
(Vivere al Limite)
11: Freak
(Capriccio)
12: It's All About POWER!
(È Tutta una Questione di POTENZA!)
13: The World Won't Stand Still
(Il Mondo non si Fermerà)
14: I Did Not See That Coming
(Non l'ho Visto Arrivare)
15: The Fisherman
(Il Pescatore)
16: All Roads Lead to Heaven or Hell
(Tutte le Strade Portano al Paradiso o all'Inferno)
17: I Don't Know You Well Enough Yet
(Non ti Conosco Ancora Abbastanza Bene)

CONTENTS

18: Patterns
(Modelli)
19: Don't Ask Any Questions
(Non Fare Domande)
20: Let's Dance
(Balliamo)
21: Create
(Creare)
22: You Can't Let Anyone Control You
(Non Puoi permettere a Nessuno di Controllarti)
23: Living Blind
(Cieco Vivente)
24: Our Dancing Styles Were Incompatible
(I Nostri Stili di Ballare Erano Incompatibili)
25: My Sanctuary
(Il Mio Santuario)
26: I'm Not Offended
(Non Sono Offeso)
27: I'm Obnoxious
(Sono Antipatico)
28: What Is Literature?
(Che Cosa è la Letteratura?)
29: Comedians Make the BEST Politicians
(I Comici Sono i Migliori Politici)
30: Mental Resistance
(Resistenza Mentale)
31: I Live in "Gaga Land"
(Io Vivo a "Gaga Land")
32: Pleasure Machine
(Macchina del Piacere)
33: Vito Mosquito
(Vito Zanzara)

CONTENTS

34: I Must Not Do Anything
(Non Devo Fare Niente)
35: Roller-coaster Blues
(Blues da Passeggiata Rullo)
36: Masturbation Blues
(Masturbazione Blues)
37: If You Put Your Mind to It...
(Se ci Metti la Mente)
38: A Pussy is a Pussy
(Una Figa è una Figa)
39: Back in Black
(Indietro nel Nero)
40: I'm an Apeman
(Sono un Uomo Scimmia)
41: Fucking
(Cazzo)
42: Pygmalion
(Pigmalione)
43: Fuck It Up
(Fanculo)
44: Free
(Libertà)
45: Blood, Flesh & Bone
(Sangue, Carne e Ossa)
46: The Men Who Sold the World
(Gli Uomini che hanno Venduto il Mondo)
47: The Man That Pissed His Shorts
(L'uomo che si è Pisciate i Pantaloncini)
48: Hassle Street
(Via della Problemi)
49: City of the Damned
(Città dei Dannati)
50: Poem With No Name
(Poesia Senza Nome)

Everything is Legal
(Tutto è Legale)

In this world.
...*everything is legal.*
...*accept if you get caught.*

"Tweeter & the Monkeyman"-Bob Dylan
Performed by-"Travelling Wilburs"

"The Don"
22.06.2023

My Grandfather, Vito Martone

(Mio Nonno, Vito Martone)

I am named after my grandfather on my mother's side...
...*Vito Martone.*
He was born in 1905 in *San Fele, Basilicata, Italy.*
I used to call him, *"Papanonna de Paese"* (grandfather father from the city),
Because...
...he lived in the village *(as opposed to my grandfather who lived on the farm)* whom I called *"Papanonno de fuori"* (grandfather from the outside).
He was a simple farmer.
He had no education.
He was illiterate...
...*he could neither read nor write.*
Yet...
...*he was a very intelligent man.*
My mother tells me many stories of her life as a little girl growing up on the farm with her sister *(who is 3 years older)* & brothers.
She paints it as an idyllic upbringing but I am sure it was not.
Because...
...*like everyone else in the region.*
...*they were very poor.*
But, I've also been told by others that knew him & they have corroborated her stories as genuine.
That....
...he was a very kind, gentle, wise & generous person.
...one who was very well liked & respected by everyone in the village.
...that his door was always open for a glass of wine.
...he had a vineyard & apparently made the best wine in the village.
One particular story my mother likes to tell me about him *(I must've heard this story a million times).*
...was when the lawyer of the village *("Avvocata Lungaressa", a stubby, fat arsehole of a man, by all accounts. You can picture the type, I'm sure).*
...stopped my grandfather in the middle of the street in the village & said,
..."Martone, se tutti fossero come te, morirei di fame!"
..."Martone, if everyone was like you, I'd die of hunger!"

Everyone knew *Vito Martone.*
Everyone LO♥ED, my grandfather, *Vito Martone.*

"The Don"
22.06.2023

Vito Martone
(My Grandfather)
(1905-1987)

MAJOR INCIDENT UNIT

(Unità per gli Incidenti Gravi)

We have received a report...
...about an incident.
...from an anonymous source.
...a very reliable, anonymous source.
...a very deep undercover anonymous source.
...although, it's not a "critical" incident.
...not yet, anyway.
...thank God for that.
...we wouldn't want this to get into the hands of the "CIU".
...FUCK no!
...not the "Critical Incident Unit".
...those "motherfuckers"!
...they're SO arrogant.
...they think that they're SO clever.
...but,
...not this time.
...not if I have anything to with it.
...they're not gonna get their dirty hands on it.
...not on my watch.

"How do you wanna handle this, Gov?"
"We have to be clever, about this."
"I want complete silence."
"Not a word must leave these walls."
"Complete secrecy & loyalty from everyone."
"That's we are going to play this."
"Otherwise, this could all go pear shaped."
"And then, we'd really be in the shit."
"I know, as a fact that "CIU", can't wait for us to fail."
"Call us amateurs."
"Leave it to the true professionals, that's what they'll love to say."
"To rub our noses & our whole bloody faces in it. If they can!"
"But we're not going to let them."
"Not this time."
"Not on my FUCKING watch, they're not!"

"The Don"
24.06.2023

Mobius

(Möbius)

Everything is *interconnected*.
Everything is *structured*.
Everything is *intertwined*.
Whatever *happens on the inside*...
...*affects what happens on the outside*.
It's designed that way.
This is "Mobius".

This is the Universe at work.
We are all part of one whole.
We are not separate Beings.
We are not disconnected from each other.
We are not detached from Nature.
We are a part of it.
Because...
...*we are Nature*.
This is "Mobius".

Social *tells us otherwise*.
Society *tells us that we are separate to each other*.
Society *pushes "Individuality"*.
Society *promotes atomisation*.
Society *wants fragmentation*.
This is wrong.
This is NOT "Mobius".

"Mobius" is *fluidity*.
"Mobius" is *interconnection*.
"Mobius" is *"Unity"*.
"Mobius" is *"Oneness"*.
"Mobius" is *"Wholeness"*.
This is "Mobius".

Be *"One"*.
Be *"Whole"*.
Be *"Interconnected"*.
Be *"Mobius"*!

"The Don"
26.06 2023

"Mobius"
Artist: Unknown

Lurking in the Shadows

(In Agguato nell'Ombra)

Who is lurking in your shadows?
Is it...
...your father who didn't want you?
...your mother that was too weak to defend & protect you?
...your brother that was the chosen one & was LO♥ED more than you?
...your sisters whom were jealous of you because they always thought that you were more beautiful than they were?
...the men who you worked for, that sabotaged your intelligence & skills?
...those you men you had that felt threatened by you force of personality?
…those women who felt betrayed by feminine power?
...the country that you were born in that couldn't handle you & exiled you?
.. your own mind which you thought you had power over & control?
Which one (a few of these) are shadows is still lurking in the shadows of your mind?

"Maybe I'm lurking somewhere in those shadows?"
"Hopefully in a "GOOD" way!"

"In the shadows of your mind."

"The Don"
26.06.2022

The Hermit

(L'eremita)

Are you a loner?
Have you decided to retreat from the world?
Maybe you have "rejected" society?
It could be for philosophical reasons?
It could be for spiritual reasons?
It could be for emotional issues?
Whichever the case...
...then you are "Hermit".

You have chosen to live…
...outside the bubble.
...outside the sphere.
...outside society.
...outside the world.

Maybe you didn't choose it...
...and it was chosen for you.
...by the Universe or some other power, we don't understand.
You are a *"Hermit"*.

In my case, I think it was the latter...
...it was chosen for me.
...by the Universe.
I had no choice in the matter.
To be...
..."The Hermit".

"The Don"
26.06.2023

I Fought the System

(Ho Combattuto il Sistema)

I fought the System...
...and the System won!

"The Don"
26.06.2023

Flatulate

(Flatulenza)

Flatuce.
Flatulency.
Flatulation.
Flatulescence.
Flatulofication.
Flatulence.
Flatuling.
Flatulific.
Flatucation.
Flatucity.
Flatulicity.
Flatulagrance.
Flatulocity.
Flatulocution.
Flatulative.
Flatulativity.
Flatulous.

"The Don"
27.06.2023

DO NOT THROW FOOD AWAY!

(NON Buttare via il Cibo!)

PLEASE...
...do NOT throw food away!
Give it away.
But...
...do NOT throw it away!

"The Don"
28.06.2023

Live on the Edge

(Vivere al Limite)

Don't take the *middle ground*.
Don't *conform*.
Don't be a *follower*.
Don't do *what everyone else is doing*.
Do be a *sheep*.
Don't be a *zombie*.
Don't he a *"walking dead"*.
Live on the edge.

Take *chances*.
Take *risks*.
Be *adventurous*.
Be a *non-conformist*.
Be a *radical*.
Be a *revolutionary*.
Live on the edge.

That's what I do.
Join me.

"Don't push me 'cause I'm close to the edge.
I'm trying not to lose my head."

-"The Message"-Grandmaster Flash & the Furious Five
Written by: Clifton Nathaniel Chase/Edward G. Fletcher/Melvin Glover/Sylvia Robinson

"The Don"
28.06.2023

Freak

(Capriccio)

Be *adventurous.*
Be *crazeeeee.*
Be *mad.*
Be *strange.*
Be *unusual.*
Be *different.*
Be *weird.*
Be *eccentric.*
Be *enigmatic.*
Be *mysterious.*
Be *yourself...*
...whomever you wanna be.
Be a FREAK.

Don't be like all the rest.
Be a FREAK.

FREAK people out!
Be a FREAK!
FREAK!
FREAK!
Be a FREAK!

FREAK!
FREAK!
Be a FREAK!
FREAK!
FREAK!
Be a FREAK!

"The Don"
28.06.2023

IT'S ALL ABOUT POWER!

(È Tutta una Questione di POTENZA!)

It's ALL about POWER!
Yep!

"The Don"
28.06.2023

The World Won't Stand Still

(Il Mondo non si Fermerà)

"And the world won't stand still".

-Trigannini"-Midnight Oil

"The Don"
28.06.2023

I Did Not See That Coming

(Non l'ho Visto Arrivare)

It took me by *surprise*.
I was *not ready*.
I didn't *expect it*.
It came from *"left field"*.
It came *"out of the blue"*.
I was *"gobsmacked"*.
I was *SHOCKED!*
I was like *"what the FUCK"*?
It caught me *unprepared*.
I was *"out of sorts"*.
I was *"all shook up"*.
I wasn't playing my *"A" game*.
I had *"dropped the ball"*.
I was *distracted*.
I was *defenceless*.
I didn't have my *eyes on the game*.
I didn't *see it coming*.
I did NOT see that coming!

"The Don"
29.06.2023

The Fisherman

(Il Pescatore)

Of the many professions...
...which is the most noble?
Is it...?
...teacher?
...the doctor?
...the policeman?
...the lawyer?
...the politician?
...the labourer?
...the scientist?
...the engineer?
...the accountant?
...the priest?

To me...
...the noblest profession of all is...
...the fisherman.

We all have to survive.
We all have to eat.
The fisherman is doing just this.
Him against Nature.
That's all.
If he's a good fisherman.
If he's skilled enough...
...he'll have dinner tonight.
If he's not...
...he'll not eat tonight.

It's a simple as this.
It couldn't be simpler.

"I wish I was a fisherman
Tumblin' on the seas
Far away from dry land
And it's bitter memories."

"Fisherman's Blues"-The Waterboys
Songwriters: Scott/Wickham

"The Don"
29.06.2023

All Roads Lead to Heaven or Hell
(Tutte le Strade Portano al Paradiso o all'Inferno)

It doesn't matter which *road you take*.
It doesn't matter which *direction you choose*.
It doesn't matter *what time you start*.
It doesn't matter *how fast or slow you travel*.
It doesn't matter *if you travel alone, with someone else or a whole army*.
It doesn't matter if you're *rich or poor*.
It doesn't matter if you are *educated or illiterate*.
It doesn't matter if you're *male, female, binary or gender neutral*.
It doesn't matter if you're *black, white or any other colour in between*.
It doesn't matter if you're a *doctor or carpenter*.
It doesn't matter if you're *young or old*.
Sooner or later, you'll realise that no matter *what you do or don't do...*
...all roads lead to Heaven or Hell.

"The Don"
01.07.2024

I Don't Know You Well Enough Yet
(Non ti Conosco Ancora Abbastanza Bene)

"I don't know you well enough you!"
That's what she said.
"It took me a year before I got together with my last boyfriend."
"WOW! That's a long time".
I replied.
"And look how that's worked out!"
"Yeh!"
She said.
"What do you wanna know?"
I replied.
"You can ask me anything you want!"

This is how it all started.

How it will end...
...is the adventure.

"The Don"
03.07.2023

Patterns

(Modelli)

There are patterns *everywhere*.
There are patterns in *everything*.
You just have to *look carefully*.
To just have to *open your eyes*.
You'll see patterns everywhere.

There are patterns in *Nature*.
There are patterns in *mathematics*.
There are patterns in *music*.
There are patterns in *science*.
There are patterns in *history*.
There are patterns in *relationships*.
There are patterns in *human behaviour*.
There are patterns in *you*.
In fact...
...*YOU are a pattern!*

Some see the *"Hand of God"* in these grand designs.
Others see the *"Universe"* at play.
Whatever it is, I definitely see intelligence in the chaos of randomness & chance.

There are patterns *everywhere*.
Just open your eyes...
...*and SEE!*

"The Don"
04.07.2023

Don't Ask Any Questions
(Non Fare Domande)

Don't ask any questions.
You might not like the answers.

"The Don"
07.07.2023

Let's Dance

(Balliamo)

You've got problems in your *life?*
You've got *stress?*
You've got issues in your *relationship?*
You've got *family issues.*
There's only one thing to do...
...*let's dance.*

You feel like you're a *loser.*
You feel like you're a *failure.*
You feel like you're a *nobody.*
You feel like you're a *"reject".*
Well...
...there's only one thing to do...
...*let's dance.*

You see *chaos everywhere you look.*
You see *politicians taking bribes on the side.*
You see *governments lying to the population.*
You see *the planet being scorched.*
Well...
...there's only one thing to do...
...*let's dance.*

Your *love life is non-existent.*
Your *social life is boring.*
Your *friends don't give a shit about you.*
Your *whole existence seems meaningless & futile.*
Well...
...there's only one thing to do...
...*let's dance.*

"Let's dance
Put on your red shoes and dance the blues
Let's dance
To the song they're playin' on the radio
Let's sway
While color lights up your face
Let's sway
Sway through the crowd to an empty space.

Let's dance
Let's dance
Let's dance, dance, dance."

Let's dance
Put on your red shoes and dance the blues
Let's sway
Under the moonlight, this serious moonlight
Let's dance
Let's dance
Let's dance, dance, dance."

-Songwriters: Doc Pomus/Mort Shuman
-Performed by: David Bowie

"The Don"
10.07.2023

(Creare)

That's ALL I can do.
Is...
...CREATE!

"The Don"
10.07.2023

You Can't Let Anyone Control You
(Non Puoi permettere a Nessuno di Controllarti)

You can't let anyone control you!
That's it!

"The Don"
10.07.2023

Living Blind

(Cieco Vivente)

*We don't know a FUCKING thing!
Because...
...we are don't FUCKING see.
Because...
...we're living blind!*

"The Don"
10.07.2023

Our Dancing Styles Were Incompatible
(I Nostri Stili di Ballare Erano Incompatibili)

She preferred a structured routine.
I, on the other hand, prefer an unstructured, free flowing style.
One that takes me wherever the music goes.
Two completely opposite forms.

Structured verses free form.
It's like as if matter & anti-matter were to come into contact.
And we know the outcome of that union.
Kabam!

Not that she wasn't any good.
In fact, she was fantastic.
A feast for the eyes, to watch her sashay her hips.

We danced a few times in the early days but we were both not completely comfortable.

She told me that I should take dancing lessons.
She didn't realise that would be like asking *Bob Dylan* to take singing lessons.

She was intellectual, patterns, routines, steps, repetition.
I was emotional, feelings, unstructured, flowing, organic, passionate.

No...
...we don't dance together anymore.

"The Don"
10.07.2023

My Sanctuary

(Il Mio Santuario)

A place of *comfort*.
A place of *protection*.
A place of *warmth*.
A place of *quite reflection*.
A place of *rejuvenation*.
A place of *escape*.
A place of *happiness*.
A place of *laughter*.
A place of *fun*.
A place of *music*.
A place of *dancing*.
A place of *rest*.
A place of *friendship*.
A place of *contemplation*.
A place of *meditation*.
A place of *serenity*.
A place of *tranquillity*.
A place of *spirituality*.
A place of *harmony*.
A place of *LO*♥*E*.
This is my place.
This is my *sanctuary*.
What is your *sanctuary*?

Earth is our *sanctuary*.

Let's not shit in our sanctuary!

"The Don"
11.07.2023

I'm Not Offended

(Non Sono Offeso)

I'm NOT offended.
Truely...
...*I'm NOT offended.*
Speak your *piece*.
Express your *opinions*.
Share your *thoughts*.
Show us your *point-of-view*.
Get it off your *chest*.
I'm NOT offended.
Truely...
...*I'm NOT offended.*

In fact, I *welcome it*.
I need to *hear this*.
I need to *absorb it*.
I need to *process this*.
Bring it on.
I'm NOT offended.
Truely...
...*I'm NOT offended.*

"The Don"
11.07.2023

I'm Obnoxious

(Sono Antipatico)

I'm *loud*.
I'm *crude*.
I'm *rude*.
I'm *arrogant*.
I'm *cringeworthy*.
I'm *irreverent*.
I'm *blasphemous*.
I'm *bombastic*.
I'm *melodramatic*.
I'm *repetitive*.
I'm *embarrassing*.
I'm a *fool*.
I'm an *idiot*.
I'm *"persona non grata"*.
I'm *"outta control"*.
I'm *NOT funny*.
I'm *mindless*
I have *NO mind*.
I'm *shameless*.
I have *NO shame*.
I'm *ridiculous*.
I'm a *trouble-maker*.
I'm a *shit-stirrer*.
I'm a *"Social misfit"*.
I'm an *entertainer (& a bad one at that)*.
I'm obnoxious.

Did I say that…
…*I'm LOUD?*
…*VERY LOUD!*

But...
…*I'm NOT a LOSER!*

"The Don"
12.07.2023

What Is Literature?

(Che Cosa è la Letteratura?)

What is "Literature"?
Well...
...to answer this question,
...we must first define what "Literature" is.
Then...
...anything that fits this criteria,
Is...
..."Literature".

"The Don"
12.07.2023

Comedians Make the BEST Politicians

(I Comici Sono i Migliori Politici)

Comedians make the BEST politicians.
Hahahahahahahaha!
Don't make me laugh!
I thought they WERE comedians!
No!
They're ARSEHOLES!
Hahahahahahahaha!
Now THAT'S funny!
Hahahahahahahaha!
Hahahahahahahaha!
Hahahahahahahaha!
Hahahahahahahaha!

"The Don"
13.07.2023

Mental Resistance

(Resistenza Mentale)

It *stops you.*
It *impedes you.*
It *frustrates you.*
Don't let it.
Break on through...
...to the other side.

"Break on through to the other side."

"The Don"
14.07.2023

I Live in "Gaga Land"

(Io Vivo a "Gaga Land")

I'm a *fantasist*.
I'm *delusional*.
I'm *self-absorbed*.
I'm *arrogant*.
I'm *lazy*.
I'm *crazy*.
I'm *mad*.
I'm *stoopid*.
I'm a *narcissist*.
I live in "Gaga Land".

I think I'm smart.
I think I'm *intelligent*.
I think I'm *handsome*.
I think I'm *SEXY!*
I think I'm an *"International man of mystery"*.
I think I'm a *poet*.
I think I'm *mystical*.
I think I'm spiritual.
I think I'm *the BEST!*
I think I'm *"Mr Smith"*.
I live in "Gaga Land".

"The Don"
15.07.2023

Pleasure Machine

(Macchina del Piacere)

I am a pleasure machine.
I pleasure you in every & any way you want.
Put in an order.
No request is too much.
No fetish is refused.
No fetish is denied.
What is your pleasure?
What is your fetish?
What are your hidden desires?
Don't be shy.
Don't be timed.
Don't be afraid.
Discretion is assured.
I will fulfil your every desire.
You will not be disappointed.
I am a true professional.
I take my job seriously.
I have soft hands.
I have a long tongue.
I never rush.
You will definitely be satisfied...
...and screaming for more.
But you'll have to wait...
...until next time.
Because...
...I am a pleasure machine.

"The Don"
16.07.2023

Vito Mosquito

(Vito Zanzara)

This is what I was called by the other kids in primary school.
"Vito Mosquito".
I hated it!

"Vito Mosquito"!
"Vito Mosquito"!
"Vito Mosquito"!
"Vito Mosquito"!
"Vito Mosquito"!
"Vito Mosquito"!

"The Don"
16.07.2023

I Must Not Do Anything

(Non Devo Fare Niente)

I must do *nothing*.
I cannot do *anything*.
I cannot *contact you*.
I must *not think that I can do anything*.
I must *refrain from making any sort of contact*.
I must *wait*.
I must *bid my time*.
I must *do nothing*.
I must *not do anything*.
But...
...sometimes...
...*it is VERY hard!*

"The Don"
16.07.2023

Roller-coaster Blues

(Blues da Passeggiata Rullo)

I've got the *"Roller-coaster Blues"*.
Over you.
I've got the *"Roller-coaster Blues"*.
Over you.
And there's nothing I can do.

I've got the *"Roller-coaster Blues"*.
I just staring at my shoes.
I've got the *"Roller-coaster Blues"*
Over you.
Because that's all I can do.

This world is turning upside down.
It's spinning me round & round.
I must have the *"Rollercoaster Blues"*, baby
Because I know that I'm going down.

Yeah, I've got the *"Roller-coaster Blues"*, baby.
It's fucking up mind.
I've got the *"Roller-coaster Blues"*, honey.
And it's making me lose my mind.

Yeah, I've got the *"Roller-coaster Blues"*, baby.
Yeah, the *"Roller-coaster Blues"*.
Yeah, I've got the *"Roller-coaster Blues"*.
And there's nothing I can do.

"The Don"
17.07.2023

Masturbation Blues

(Masturbazione Blues)

I'm old, I'm cold.
There's nothing I can do about it.
Except...
...spank the monkey.
...jerk the turk.
...fool with the tool.
...fizz the jizz.
...blow my cool.
But...
...I'm 64
...and I can't get it up anymore.
I've got the *masturbation blues...*
...again.

Let's give it another go.
Let's give it one more try.
You know what they say...
..."Use it or lose it".
I don't want to lose it.
I've still got a lot of jizz to give.
So...
...I psych myself.
I can do this.
I've got this.
I can't let the team down.
I get down to work.
But...
...all my work's in vain.
There's no happy ending today.
Because...
...I'm 64
...and I can't get it up anymore.
I've got the *masturbation blues...*
...again.

I've got the *masturbation blues...*
...again.

"The Don"
18.07.2023

If You Put Your Mind to It...
(Se ci Metti la Mente)

If you put your mind to it...
...you can do ANYTHING!
Well...
...maybe...
...not everything.
How about?
If you put your mind to it...
...you can do a lot of things.
That's better.
More realistic.
Let's not get carried away with those phonie positive platitudes...
...that only end up in failure.
Now don't get me wrong...
...I'm a very positive guy & I encourage one to challenge oneself.
But...
...let's be realistic here.
What are your chances of becoming...
...an astronaut?
Or a...
...movie star?
Don't be *sold a pack of lies.*
Don't be *gullible.*
Don't be *delusional.*
Just accept that...
...really...
If you put your mind to it...
...they'll only be a few things you can do!

Don't be *sold "False Hopes".*

"The Don"
19.07.2023

A Pussy is a Pussy

(Una Figa è una Figa)

For a man...
...a pussy is a pussy.
....no matter who it belongs to.
We don't discriminate.
Any pussy will do.
Because...
...a pussy is a pussy.

A pussy is a pussy.
A pussy is a pussy.
A pussy is a pussy.
A pussy is a pussy.

"The Don"
19.07.2023

Back in Black

(Indietro nel Nero)

Why is *"Black"* so *coveted?*
Why is *"Black"* so *sought after?*
Why is *"Black"* so *desirable?*
Why is *"Black"* so *"COOL"*?

Does it have anything to do with...
...making you look...
...*more desirable?*
...*more independent?*
...*more available?*
...*more notorious?*
...*more BAD?*
...*more NAUGHTY?*
...*more SINFUL?*
....*more DEADLY?*
...*more SEXY?*
...*more FUCKABLE?*

Maybe?

"'Cause I'm back
Yes, I'm back
Well, I'm back
Yes, I'm back
Well, I'm back, back
Well, I'm back in black
Yes, I'm back in black."

-"Back in Black"-AC/DC
-Written by: A. Young/B. Johnson/M. Young

"The Don"
21.07.2023

I'm an Apeman

(Sono un Uomo Scimmia)

I am *feral*.
I am *wild*.
I'm an *animal*.
I am *primal*.
I am a *primate*.
I am a *gorilla*.
I am *untameable*.
I *cannot be tamed*.
Because...
...*I am an APEMAN!*

I *swing through the trees*.
I *wear no clothes*.
I *never wash*.
I *smell like nature*.
I am *a child of Nature*.
I am *savage*.
I am *crazy*.
I am *SHOCKING!*
I am *SHAMELESS!*
I am *TERRIBLE!*
Because...
...*I am an APEMAN!*

I don't talk...
...*I grunt.*
...*l roar.*
...*l shout.*
...*l scream.*
...*l yell.*
...*l like to fuck "doggy style"!*

I am *scary*.
I am *terrifying*.
Don't stand in my way...
...because...
...I am an APEMAN!

"I'm an apeman, I'm an ape, apeman, oh I'm an apeman
I'm a King Kong man, I'm a voodoo man, oh I'm an apeman.

I don't feel safe in this world no more
I don't want to die in a nuclear war
I want to sail away to a distant shore and make like an apeman.

I'm an apeman, I'm an ape, apeman, oh I'm an apeman
I'm a King Kong man, I'm a voodoo man, oh I'm an apeman."

-*"Apeman"-The Kinks*
-Songwriter: Ray Davies

"The Don"
24.07.2023

Fucking

(Cazzo)

Fucking is...
...*primitive.*
Fucking is...
...*primordial*
Fucking is...
...*animalistic.*
Fucking is...
...*organic.*
Fucking is...
...*naturalistic.*
Fucking is...
...*orgasmic.*
Fucking is...
...*euphoric.*
Fucking is...
...*religious.*
Fucking is...
...*spiritual.*
Fucking is...
...*divine.*
Fucking is...
...*Heavenly*
Fucking is...
...*FREEDOM.*
Fucking is...
...*BEAUTIFUL.*
Fucking is...
...*HUMAN.*
Fucking is...
...*sexual.*
Fucking can be...
...*LO♥E (if you're with the RIGHT person).*

So...

...let's FUCK!

Pygmalion

(Pigmalione)

Have you the story of *"Pygmalion"*?
Well, basically it's about a man that wants to transform a girl...
...into someone he desires.
He changes her *hair*.
He changes her *clothes*.
He changes her *looks*.
He changes the way she *walks*.
He changes the way she *talks*.
He changes EVERYTHING *about her*.
Even...
...her PERSONALITY!

But one thing he didn't take into account...
...one thing he didn't take into consideration.
Was...
...her BEING!
...her HUMANITY!

Some might call it...
...her SOUL.

It doesn't matter what you call it.
It that internal *"Thing"* that makes one intrinsically & innately *"YOU"*!

This can NEVER be manipulated!

"The Don"
24.07.2023

Fuck It Up

(Fanculo)

Fuck it up...
...you know you're gonna do it.
Fuck it up...
...you know you're gonna screw it.
Fuck it up...
...you know you're gonna blow it.
Fuck it up...
...you know you're gonna kill it.
Fuck it up...
...you know you're gonna fail it.
Fuck it up...
...you know you're gonna ruin it.
Fuck it up...
...you know you're gonna hate it.
Fuck it up...
...you know you're gonna lose it.
Fuck it up...
...you know you're gonna throw it.
Fuck it up...
...you know you're gonna destroy it.
Fuck it up...
...you know you're gonna consume it.
Fuck it up...
...you know you're gonna subsume it.
Fuck it up...
...you know you're gonna spew it.
Fuck it up...
...you know you're gonna suck it.
Fuck it up...
...you know you're gonna fuck it.

Fuck it up...
...you know you're gonna do it.
Fuck it up...
...you know you're gonna do it.
Fuck it up...
...you know you're gonna...
Fuck it up...
...you know you're gonna...
Fuck it up...
...you know you're gonna...
Fuck it up...
...you know you're gonna...

Fuck it up!

"The Don"
26.07.2023

(Libertà)

We are NOT free.
Someday, maybe...
...we WILL be free.
But...
...today is NOT that day.
When will that day arrive?
Will it be soon?
Will it EVER arrive?
That day...
...when we will ALL be free?

Today we are *NOT free.*
We are *prisoners.*
We are *slaves.*
We are *in chains.*
To the "SYSTEM"!

But...
...one day.
...maybe.
...we WILL be free.
But...
...today is NOT that day!
Today, we are NOT free!
But...
...someday we WILL be FREE!

Maybe…
...if we're lucky!

"The Don"
26.07.2023

Blood, Flesh & Bone
(Sangue, Carne e Ossa)

Blood, flesh & bone.
We are MORE than JUST blood, flesh & bone!

"The Don"
26.07.07.2023

The Men Who Sold the World

(Gli Uomini che hanno Venduto il Mondo)

The men who sold the World.
Who are these men?
Why do they hide behind masks?
The masks of civility?
The mask of society?
The mask of servitude?
The mask of humanity?
When in fact...
...they are EVIL men.
...men who are destroying the planet.
...men who are destroying society.
...men who are destroying or dignity.
...men who are destroying our HUMANITY.
Who are these men...?
...these men who sold the World?

Is "Elon Musk" one of these men?

Oh SHIT...
...we're FUCKED!

"The Don"
26.07.2023

The Man That Pissed His Shorts

(L'uomo che si è Pisciate i Pantaloncini)

I stupidly looked down at his crutch.
He was wearing shorts.
I noticed that he had wet himself.
I sang a song to him, *"Why did you piss your pants?"*
He looked at me & said, *"I always piss myself because I can't stop pissing"*.
He stood there in front of me proudly showing his pissed shorts.
He was not ashamed or embarrassed.
"You should wear nappies", I said.
"In case of such emergencies".
It's a well known biological fact, that as people get older *(especially men)*,
they start to suffer from *"partial loss of bladder control"*.

In other words, they suffer from leakages, *(they piss themselves)*.
So, to avoid embarrassing situations such as these there are *"Incontinence Pads"* which you can buy that absorb the piss.
They act just like nappies on a baby.
The only difference is that these are nappies for old people.

The circle of life is a curious phenomenon.
We are born babies, live, get old & become babies again.

Off he goes back to work with not a care in world.
People walk past seeing him with his wet pants but he goes back work on his mail delivery.
Without a care in the world.
But...
...I know!
...I see his wet pants.
...I know that he pissed himself.
...and that's ALL that matters.

But he was happy, singing an *"Elvis"* song as we walked away.
"I'm just a hunk, hunk of burning love.
I'm just a hunk, hunk of burning love".
He was a damn good *"Elvis"* impersonator.

I saw him a couple of days later & he shouts to me from across the road,
"I'm wearing nappies!".
"Good to know!", I reply.

"I'm just a hunk, hunk of burning love.
I'm just a hunk, hunk of burning love".

"The Don" + JLo
26.07.2023

Hassle Street

(Via della Problemi)

You've got to haggle...
...on Hassle Street.
You've got to barter...
...on Hassle Street.
You've got to roll...
...on Hassle Street.
You've got to flow...
...on Hassle Street.
You've got to struggle...
...on Hassle Street.
You've got to fight...
...on Hassle Street.
You've got to run...
...on Hassle Street.
You've got to negotiate...
...on Hassle Street.
You've got to argue...
...on Hassle Street.
You've got to beg...
...on Hassle Street.
You've got to hustle...
...on Hassle Street.
You've got to hassle...
...on Hassle Street.

You can't stroll...
...on Hassle Street.
Hassle Street.
...on Hassle Street.
Hassle Street.
...on Hassle Street.
Hassle Street.

"The Don"
28.07.2023

City of the Damned

(Città dei Dannati)

Have you heard of the *"Village of the damned"*?
A place where all the rejects of society were taken.

The *sick.*
The *feeble.*
The *deformed.*
The *anarchists.*
The *revolutionaries.*
The *rebellious.*
The *"non-conformists".*
The so called *"social misfits".*
The *"anti-establishments".*
The *activists.*
The *artists.*
The *intellectuals.*
The *philosophers.*
The *miscreants.*
The *enquirers.*
The *mavericks.*
The *dissidents.*
The *malcontents.*
The *"social" agitators.*

Those that questioned the social & political order of the day.

They were all rounded up & taken to the *"Village of the Damned"...*
...if they were not killed first.
They were kept isolated & separated from the rest of the so called *"civilised"* society.

Hard to believe but it still exists today. But now it is no longer just a village...
...it has grown to become a city.
...a "Megalopolis"!
It is called...
..."City of the Damned"!

Some might even say that this city has spread across the entire planet.
That...
...we are all DAMNED!
We all live in a *"City of the Damned"*!
But...
...we don't know it!

"The Don"
29.07.2023

Poem With No Name

(Poesia Senza Nome)

This poem has no name.
It doesn't need one.
The words speak for themselves.
They say everything you need to know.
They contain the meaning.
There is no hidden message.
There is no underlying subtext.
There is no ambiguity.
There is no hidden code.
The words are there in black & white.
Everything you need to know is there.
The words tell the story.
The words carry the meaning.
The poem is a very simple one.
It has a very simple message.
The poem doesn't need a name.
The poem speaks for itself.

It's all about LO♥E, DEATH & everything else in between.

It's ALL been said before anyway!

That's why this poem has no name.
Because...
...it doesn't need one.

"The Don"
30.07.2023

Books written by "The Don"

"My Life with Chickens & other stories: I Pity the Poor Immigrant"
Published:
10th September, 2019
Autobiography Book 1:
0 – 12 years old

"Poems for Misfits, Miscreants, Misanthropes, Mavericks, Losers & Malcontents!"
Published:
10th June, 2020
Book of Poems 1

"Poems for Troubled Minds & Trouble Hearts"
Published:
10th August, 2020

Book of Poems 2

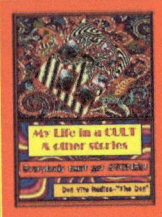

"My Life in a CULT & other stories: Everybody Must Get STONED!"
Published:
10th September, 2020
Autobiography Book 2:
15 – 30 years old

"Poems for Restless Minds & Restless Hearts"
Published:
10th October, 2020
Book of Poems 3

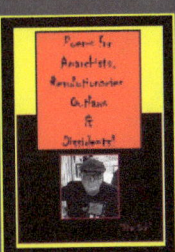

"Poems for Anarchists, Revolutionaries, Outlaws & Dissidents!"
Published:
10th November, 2020

Book of Poems 4

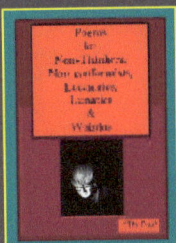

"Poems for Non-Thinkers & Eccentrics"
Published:
10th December, 2020
Book of Poems 5

"The Rantings of a Madman"
Published:
10th January, 2021

Book of Poems 6

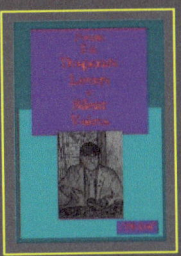

"Poems for Desperate Lovers & Silent Voices"
Published:
10th February, 2021
Book of Poems 7

"Poems for Tormented Minds & Tortured Souls"
Published:
10th March, 2021
Book of Poems 8

All available ONLY online

Books written by "The Don"

"Poems for ALIENS, Outsiders, Outcasts & other STRANGE BEINGS!"
Published: 10th April, 2021
Book of Poems 9

"Poems for Beings From Another Planet"
Published: 10th May, 2021
Book of Poems 10

"Poems for Mindless Beings & Lost Souls"
Published: 10th June, 2021
Book of Poems 11

"Poems for the Broken Hearted & Misunderstood
Published: 10th July, 2021
Book of Poems 12

"Poems for Poems for the Bewildered, Dazed & Confused"
10th August, 2021
Book of Poems 13

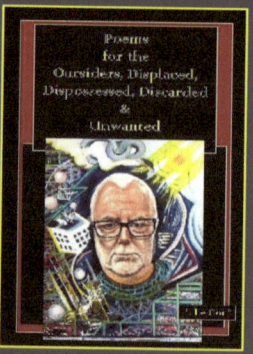

"Poems for the Outsiders, Displaced, Dispossessed, Discarded & Unwanted"
Published: 10th Sept, 2021
Book of Poems 14

All available ONLY online

"Poems for Secret Agents, Phantom Agents, Agents of Change, Agent Provocateurs & Agents of Chaos"
Published: 10th Oct, 2021
Book of Poems 15

"Poems for Disenchanted, Disillusioned & Delusional"
Published: 10th November, 2021
Book of Poems 16

Books written by "The Don"

"Poems for the Stoners, drugos, ACID takers & Psychedelic LO♥ERS (Everybody Must Get Stoned)"
Published: 10th December, 2021
Book of Poems 17

"Poems for Anarchists, Rebels & Revolutionaries
Published: 10th January, 2022
Book of Poems 18

"Poems for Rebels, Radicals & Revolutionaries (Viva la Révolution!)"
Published: 10th February, 2022
Book of Poems 19

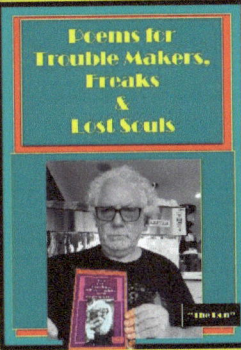

"Poems for Trouble Makers, Freaks & Lost Souls"
Published: 10th March 2022
Book of Poems 20

"Poems for Zombies & the Walking Dead"
Published: 10th April 2022
Book of Poems 21

"Poems for Non-Conformists (Never conform!)"
Published: 10th May 2022
Book of Poems 22

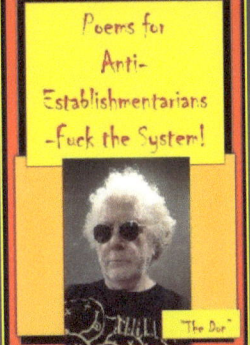

"Poems for Anti-Establishment-arians -Fuck the System!"
Published: 10th June 2022
Book of Poems 23

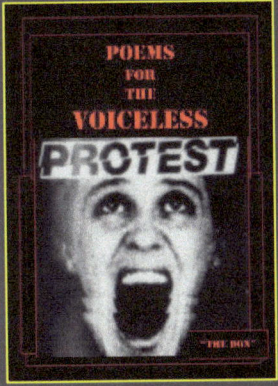

"Poems for the Voiceless"
Published: 10th July 2022
Book of Poems 24

All available ONLY online

Books written by "The Don"

"Poems for the Fearless"

Published: 10th August 2022

Book of Poems 25

"Poems for the PEACEMAKER: Make peace NOT war!"

Published: 10th March 2023

Book of Poems 26

Poems for the Forever Young (May you stay forever young!)
Published: 10th June 2023
Book of Poems 27

Poems for the Children of the REVOLUTION!
Published: 5th December 2023

Book of Poems 28

All available ONLY online

Poems for the L'Innocente!
Published:
1st January 2024
Book of Poems 29

Poems for the IMMORTALS (They who die before they die will never die!)
Published: 10th March 2024
Book of Poems 30

www.ingramcontent.com/pod-product-compliance
Lightning Source LLC
Chambersburg PA
CBHW042048290426
44109CB00006B/148